D1572643

By Charles Simic

RETURN TO A
PLACE LIT BY
A GLASS OF MILK

THE BRAZILLER SERIES OF POETRY
Richard Howard, General Editor

RETURN TO A PLACE LIT BY A GLASS OF MILK

Poems by

CHARLES SIMIC

GEORGE BRAZILLER

New York

Some of these poems have previously appeared in the following publications, to whose editors grateful acknowledgment is made: *Antaeus, Arion's Dolphin, Boundary, Cafe Solo, The California Quarterly, Crazy Horse, Epoch, Field, The First Issue, Isthmus, Kayak, Land at the Tip of the Hair, Lillabulero, The New Yorker, The Ohio Review, Open Reading, Poetry, The Seneca Review, Some, Sumac, The Unmuzzled Ox. I also wish to thank the John Simon Guggenheim Memorial Foundation for a grant which paid my rent and food while this book was being written.*

Standard Book Number: 0-8076-0732-0, cloth
0-8076-0733-9, paper
Library of Congress Catalog Card Number: 73-92763
First Printing
Printed in the United States of America
Designed by Harry Ford and Kathleen Carey

To all my friends

Contents

I

II

III

IV

V

I

Aunt Lettuce, I want to look under your skirt.

THE BIRD

A bird calls me
From an apple tree
In the midst of sleep.

Calls me from the pink twig of daylight,
From the top of a shadow with roots
That grow each night closer to my heart,
From the steeple of a white cloud.

I give her my sleep,
She dyes it red.
I give her my breath,
She turns it into rustling leaves.

In the throat of that unknown bird
There's a vowel of my name.

She calls me from the talons of the morning star,
She calls me from the nest of the morning mist,
That chirp, like a burning candle
On a windy threshold.

*

Bird, shaped
Like the insides
Of a yawning
Mouth.

Now your voice touches me even more tenderly,
Tracing its hushed trajectory

At five in the morning
When the sky turns cold and lucent
Like the water in which
They baptized a small child.

*

I started on the thread
Of the bird's whistle,
Naked,
Climbing like smoke.

The earth grew smaller underneath.
My bare feet touched
The chill coming from the north.

Later, I fell
In a field of nettles
And dreamt I had
The eyes of that bird,

Watching from the heights,
How the roads meet
And part once again.

TRAVELLING

I turn myself into a sack.
An old ragpicker
Takes me out at dawn.
We go shuffling, we go stooped.

Here he says is the blue tie,
A man climbed it as it hung from his neck.
He's up there sobbing now
For he doesn't know how to come down.

But I say nothing, what can a sack say?

Here he says is the overcoat.
His name is Ahab, his tatters are our tatters.
He is searching for the tailor who made him.
He wants all his black threads ripped out.

But I say nothing, what can a sack say?

Here he says are the boots,
As they sunk, as they went under
They saw their lives in a flash,
They'll cling to us wherever we go.

*But I say nothing, what can a sack
Stuffed to its throat say?*

PAIN

What would I do
Without you
My seamstress you
With a needle in your mouth
Swift as a bee's sting

Sew stitch
These body rags
With the last thread of
Daylight sing them
Into wedding-clothes

You and me and the lamp
The house like a nest
Our mother bluebird long gone
Our father falcon hunting

What would I do
Without you without
Your voice
That names and names
The streams and rivers
Of our days on earth.

MOTHER TONGUE

Sold by a butcher
Wrapped in a newspaper
It travels in a bag
Of the stooped widow
Next to some onions and potatoes

Toward a dark house
Where a cat will
Leap off the stove
Purring
At its entrance.

SECOND AVENUE WINTER

When the horses were no longer found in dreams,
And the country virgins ceased riding them naked.
When their manes ceased to resemble sea-foam,
And the twitching of their ears no longer prophesied
    great battles.

Just then, a horse came pulling a wagon
Piled up high with old mattresses,
Bent under a grey army blanket
On thick sturdy legs the color of winter's twilight,
Partly a ghost, partly a poor man's burial,
Bringing with each step the heaviness
Of a dumb and unknown animal sorrow.

The fresh snow sobbed under the hoofs of the last horse.
The wagon wheels whined their ancient lineage
Of country roads, of drunks left lying in the mud—
A million years of shivering and coughing.

I too went after them
With a slow shuffle
Of sweet sanctified thoughts,
Like a bearded pilgrim.

Thinking of the old negro driver,
Of the insanity that makes him keep
A horse in New York city,
Of their night and their supper,
Its ritual and secret life
Where I wish to be anointed.

1968

9

SONG

There's a house on the tip of a branch.
It sways in the Summer breeze.
The great tree won't let it fall
Even when the wind comes to shake it.

Its only door is a beak. It opens
To steal the starlight. Inside
You can see the ribs. It's a house so tiny
It can fit in the dark of my eye.

When I close that eye, I can hear the sea in the other.
It bears the house through the night.
With my tongue I touch its prow from within,
With my breath I blow
The candles in the captain's cabin.

When sleep overtakes me,
I say good-by to the house.
I lower onto my heart
All that it cannot ferry on.

WATERMELONS

Green Buddhas
On the fruit stand.
We eat the smile
And spit out the teeth.

ARTICHOKES

for Bob Williams

I have two roosters
Buried in my backyard,
Two roosters pecking
Under the earth,
Only their green tails showing.

And they turn,
These two weathervanes,
Inching their
Saw-toothed shadows,

A log of twilight,
A log of sunlight
Sawed clean. Dew
Trickling down
To that blacksmith's anvil
Where their lances
And shields are hammered.

Vegetables,
Readying themselves
For the battlefield,
For that summer night
When the moon is worn
Like a sleeve at the elbow,
And my window turned
Toward the Pacific
Needs ancient sentries,

For the oil dozing
With one eye open
In its bottle, for
The cleft-footed garlic
Hung by a nail, for
The salt and pepper
Weighing the house down
Against the storms
That are coming . . .

Until that time, that supper
Immaculate and solemn,
When they'll shed their armor
And place on each plate
Between the fork and the knife
The lost heart of Saint Francis
Lover of birds
In a wreath of thorns.

SOLITUDE

There now, where the first crumb
Falls from the table
You think no one hears it
As it hits the floor

But somewhere already
The ants are putting on
Their Quakers' hats
And setting out to visit you.

II

I may be blind, but I got my eye on you.
Paul Shapiro

THE STORY

About a fly
Which is not
A fly

About its swift
Powerful wings
Which do not exist

About its eyes
Which remain behind
In winter

Its eggs which
The epicureans
Consider a delicacy

Its bite which
Is painful
And equally imaginary

The art of plucking
Its nonexistent legs
One by one

Fortune-telling
With a sugar-cube
As its bait

How I drank
Its corpse
In a glass of milk

And caught
Its shadow
On the flypaper of my tongue.

WATCH REPAIR

A small wheel
Incandescent,
Shivering like
A pinned butterfly.

Hands
Pointing in all directions:
The crossroads
One enters
In a nightmare.

Higher than anyone
Number 12 presides
Like a beekeeper
Over the swarming honeycomb
Of the open watch.

—Other wheels
That could fit
Inside a raindrop,

Tools
That must be splinters
Of arctic starlight . . .

Tiny golden mills
Grinding invisible
Coffee beans.

When the coffee's boiling,
Cautiously,
So it doesn't burn us,

We raise it
To the lips
Of the nearest
Ear.

BROOMS

for Tomaz, Susan and George

I

Only brooms
Know the devil
Still exists,

That the snow grows whiter
After a crow has flown over it,
That a dark dusty corner
Is the place of dreamers and children,

That a broom is also a tree
In the orchard of the poor,
That a hanging roach there
Is a mute dove.

2

Brooms appear in dreambooks
As omens of approaching death.
This is their secret life.
In public, they act like flat-chested old maids
Preaching temperance.

They are sworn enemies of lyric poetry.
In prison they accompany the jailer,
Enter cells to hear confessions.
Their short-end comes down
When you least expect it.

Left alone behind a door
Of a condemned tenement,
They mutter to no one in particular,
Words like *virgin wind moon-eclipse,*
And that most sacred of all names:
Hieronymous Bosch.

3

In this and in no other manner
Was the first ancestral broom made:
Namely, they plucked all the arrows
From the bent back of Saint Sebastian.
They tied them with a rope
On which Judas hung himself.
Stuck in the stilt
On which Copernicus
Touched the morning star . . .

Then the broom was ready
To leave the monastery.
The dust welcomed it—
That great pornographer
Immediately wanted to
Look under its skirt.

4

The secret teaching of brooms
Excludes optimism, the consolation
Of laziness, the astonishing wonders
Of a glass of aged moonshine.

It says: the bones end up under the table.
Bread-crumbs have a mind of their own.
The milk is you-know-who's semen.
The mice have the last squeal.

As for the famous business
Of levitation, I suggest remembering:
There is only one God
And his prophet is Mohammed.

5

And then finally there's your grandmother
Sweeping the dust of the nineteenth century
Into the twentieth, and your grandfather plucking
A straw out of the broom to pick his teeth.

Long winter nights.
Dawns a thousand years deep.
Kitchen windows like heads
Bandaged for toothache.

The broom beyond them sweeping,
Tucking the lucent grains of dust
Into neat pyramids,
That have tombs in them,

Already sacked by robbers,
Once, long ago.

POEM

The enigma of the invisible is the enigma
of memory. The invisible is precisely that
which no one remembers. Like that song you
used to know, like that joke that brought
tears into your eyes once . . .

And you say, once upon a time these trees
were not like these trees, once upon a time
these trees in the wind were much more
trees than these trees are . . .

But then language of course is a kind of
lullaby.

TWO RIDDLES

Hangs by a thread—
Whatever it is. Stripped naked.
Shivering. Human. Mortal.
On a thread finer than starlight.

By a power of a feeling,
Hangs, impossible, unthinkable,
Between the earth and the sky.
I, it says. I. I.

And how it boasts,
That everything that is to be known
About the wind
Is being revealed to it as it hangs.

*

It goes without saying . . .
What does? No one knows.
Goes mysterious, ah funereal,
Goes for the hell of it.

If it has an opinion,
It keeps it to itself.
If it brings tidings,
It plays dumb, plays dead.

No use trying to pin it down.
It's elusive, of a retiring habit,
In a hurry of course, scurrying—
A blink of an eye and it's gone.

All that's known about it,
Is that it goes goes
Without saying.

NOTHING

I want to see it face to face,
And then, I intend to raise hell.
No, I don't have anything prepared.
I will rely entirely on inspiration,
Also on my ancestors who just now
Begin to laugh their heads off.

In all probability I'll make a fool of myself,
Turn away grinning stupidly,
Light a cigarette with trembling fingers,
Ask about the weather, about that cloud
Shaped like a medicine bundle, hovering
So still, in the windless sky.

SOLVING THE RIDDLE

The cloud's a clue. The breeze.
Two elm trees looking suspicious.

Whose clues. My clues,
All my crafty clues,
All my strings of omens,
It's time we solve this riddle.

Clue sits. Omen flaps its wings.
They make one hand unearn
What the other earns.

*

I have a feud with my lifeline.
I take note of its crossroads and ditches.
I travel crucified.

I go solving with my ears.
The ears hear what's not there.
I go solving with my eyes.
The eyes see what everybody else sees.

*

Round, round
So that it rolls easily away,
Rolls laughing,
Shedding its skins, its doll's dresses.

White, so that it hides
Cleverly in all this snow,
And I believe it lost,
I believe it never was.

Heavy, so that I feel
Its weight on my shoulders,
My back that bends,
My foot that hesitates.

*

What is it that was under my nose
And is no more?
Did it go home?
Did it meet its old sweetheart?

I hear the emptiness where it went.
I've seen its bird-tracks
Inside my hand. I feel its absence.
Without it, I barely want to live.

It will be here tomorrow,
Disguised, hard to recognize.
I keep its bone.
I keep its chipped bowl.

*

We say good-by
My most precious clue and I.
Two question marks.
Two asses' ears.

Around a riddle
Which yields no answer
We made our nest
Of straw and matches.

The night fell quickly.

Inside my empty bottle
I was constructing a lighthouse
While all the others
Were making ships.

How to the invisible
I hired myself to learn
Whatever trade it might
Consent to teach me.

How the invisible
Came out for a walk
On a certain evening
Casting the shadow of a man.

How I followed behind
Dragging my body
Which is my tool box,
Which is my sustenance,

For a long apprenticeship
That has as its last
And seventh rule:
The submission to chance.

THE POINT

This is the story
Afraid to go on.

This is the iron cradle
Of the stillness
That rocks the story
Afraid to go on.

How it regrets
The loss of its purity,
The madness of this
Single burnt consonant,

Which now sits,
Shy, solitary,
Among all these
White spaces.

*

And it dreams,
The story afraid to go on.

In its dream it builds itself
In the shape
Of the gallows-tree.

When the gallows are completed,
It hangs by the neck
What's left of its dreamings.

Underneath, in the dirt
The shadow of its beginning
Comes to nibble
Its quivering feet.

*

There's no point,
Says the story
Afraid to go on.

It's all a question
Of the mote
In your eye.

It watches
As you watch.

Perhaps this evening
Reflects its final blackness,
Reflects its final mourning

Before it dissolves
Into a tear?

*

After its death
They opened the story
Afraid to go on.
And found nothing.

Inside nothing
They found a slip
Of the tongue.
Inside the tongue
A loose hair.
Inside the hair,
They found

Whatever
Is destroyed
Each time
It is named.

III

THE WEDDING

Mother gives me
To the daylight on the threshold.

I have the steam of my breath
For a carnation.

Poverty, my bride,
You have the lightest step.

*

Who dressed the bride?
I said the eye
As I gazed at the sky.

Who brought her here?
I said the tongue
With my bitter-tip.

Who'll see her lie?
Not you nor I,
Said the hands,
Will see her lie.

*

And what does he wear?

Something new, something worn,
Something borrowed, something stolen,

And a keen blade
Of a knife
In her glass slipper.

*

Mother makes a ring
Of bread-crust,

Wraps it in her loneliness
Instead of a napkin,

Gives it to a fly
To bring it to church.

The church is far
And its bleached graveyard.

*

Star-light, star-bright,
Last star I see this morning,
Don't breathe now
I'm kissing an emptiness
A thousand years long.

PORNOGRAPHER'S PSALM

Death has a cock that is always erect.
It writes on the wind. It writes in beautiful longhand:
    Spread your legs tonight, Martha.
    By the light of their thighs I'll come to you.
    Unbutton your dress Miss Hannum
    And bare your old maid's breasts.
    Tonight I'll spill my sperm, my rosary of worms
        on their nipples.
    And you little girl, I'll wear a hair from your
        maidenhead
    Among the grey bristles inside my left ear.

Those made pregnant by death
Have the scars of its love-making wound in black.
Their friends shuffle behind carrying wreaths.
They are drunk like wedding guests.

Death's children
Resemble you and me,
They go coughing, yes sir, they sit
In furnished rooms
When the lights are low
Adding up angels on a pinpoint,
Only to pass the time,
And the time passes.

CHARLES SIMIC

Charles Simic is a sentence.
A sentence has a beginning and an end.

Is he a simple or compound sentence?
It depends on the weather,
It depends on the stars above.

What is the subject of the sentence?
The subject is your beloved Charles Simic.

How many verbs are there in the sentence?
Eating, sleeping and fucking are some of its verbs.

What is the object of the sentence?
The object, my little ones,
Is not yet in sight.

And who is writing this awkward sentence?
A blackmailer, a girl in love,
And an applicant for a job.

Will they end with a period or a question mark?
They'll end with an exclamation point and an ink spot.

Buck has a headache. Tony ate
a real hot pepper. Sylvia weighs
herself naked on the bathroom
scale. Gary owes $800 to the
Internal Revenue. Roger says
poetry is the manufacture of lightning-rods.
José wants to punch his wife
in the mouth. Ted's afraid
of his own shadow. Ray talks
to his tomato plants. Paul
wants a job in the post office
selling stamps. Mary keeps
smiling at herself in the mirror.

And I,
I piss in the sink
with a feeling of
eternity.

STRICTLY FOR POSTERITY

Brothers, my teeth hurt
And I've no money to have them pulled.
If you know a way, tell me.

The collection man knocks on my window.
My wife sleeps with her thighs bare.
In my time I attempted a few prayers.
If you know a way, tell me.

No special identifying marks.
My coat is torn.
The wind's cold even for a dog.
My coat is still torn.

What next? I make journeys
(mostly in my thoughts),
I go back to 1942.
There's no money there either.

Here, I'll pour one shot for me,
One for this snowy night.
If I get through my 33rd year,
I'll live forever.

GEORGE SIMIC

1

Captain,
what are you doing
with that cane?
There are no dogs here anymore.
The blind-alley has eyes now.
Did you carve it from our threshold
while the new owners slept?
You are its father too;
it skips ahead of you, chattering.
When a hump grew on your back,
a shadow came to be its sister.

2

Like a fisherman, alone
on a quiet autumn lake:
the smoke of your cigar—
has the thought bitten?
I give you back the hair I stole
from your sleeping ear.
It has grown, hollow.
Blow on it as you would
on a layer of fine dust,
whistle back our old life.

3

That in you which belongs
to your mother playing the accordion,
that in me which belongs
to a glass of wine raised in your hand . . .
I hired my voice
to its sheen.
No one dies there,
no one walks alone.
The bullet they fire is white,
so is our wound.

4

If you sing now,
the table will lift itself.
If you sing now,
a beautiful woman will bare her breast.
Such clarity, it is a lens
to see far with eyes shut:
three meadows and no shadow to be found,
three meadows only one barren pear tree
like a mourner
left at the gravesite.

5

Who did we hire out to?
Who sent us early one morning,
hunger's own hirelings,
for that kettle of lentils
simmering on the stove,
for the rooster crowing at the kitchen window?
A story of footprints
that came to an end abruptly:
a place without landmarks,
a place for great dreamers.

6

Now I want to see the cleft-
footed one, the one with pig's ears,
the son of a bitch who washes
his ass in our milk, who annoints us
in his bile on the sly,
who on all evidence doesn't exist.
In the name of our sacred right
to our own madness, in the name
of our brotherhood of fear,
I want to spit over my shoulder.

7

We spoke of winters,
snowbound travellers.
We spoke of fires
neither dead nor alive.
Dawn came, dawn of laborers:
the coffee's steam was visible.
You've been gone long, old man.
With whom do you cut cards,
dog-eared, greasy cards,
black on both sides?

THE PILLOW

Are we still travelling?
Whiteness, you came out of a dog's mouth
On a cold day. Apron,
I lie within you like an apple.

You've lit up my forest. Two
Black winds you sell. Do you still
Guard me from robbers
On the road fearsome and lonesome?

To tie my breath inside you
Into a knot—find the way
Back to your old scent—
It still hasn't bought me a mockingbird.

We separated, sacred time.
I stretch between two chairs. Recently
I started wearing blinders. One-legged,
Since there's no room for the other.

The dead love eggs. This is
That stone tucked beneath you
Speaking. Bared now,
For those who grind their teeth in sleep

To lay down their heads.

IV

THE BODY

This last continent
Still to be discovered.

My hand is dreaming, is building
Its ship. For crew it gathers
A pack of bones, for food
The time alloted to them in this life.

It knows the breath that blows north.
With the breath from the west
It will sail east each night.

The scent of your body as it sleeps
Is the land-birds sighted at sea.

My touch is on the highest mast.
It cries at four in the morning
As one of your thighs turns white
On the rim of the world.

BALLAD

What's that approaching like dusk like poverty
A little girl picking flowers in a forest
The migrant's fire of her long hair
Harm's way she comes and also the smile's round about way

In another life in another life
Aunt rain sewing orphan's buttons to each stone
Solitude's stitch
Let your horns out little stone

Screendoor screeching in the wind
Mother-hobble-gobble baking apples
Wooden spoons dancing ah the idyllic life of wooden spoons
I need a table to spread these memories on

Little girl fishing using me as bait
Me a gloomy woodcutter in the forest of words
I am going to say one thing and mean another
I'll tuck you in a matchbox like a hornet

In another life in another life
Dandelion and red poppy grow in the back yard
Shoes in the rain bark at the milkman
Little girl alone playing blindman's buff

The words want to bring back more—
You are *it* she says laughing and is gone
Divination by one's own heartbeat
Draw near to what doesn't say yes or no

And she had nothing under her dress
Star like an eye the gamecocks have overlooked
Tune up your fingers and whistle
On a trail lined with elms she hides herself behind a tree

I tread the sod you walked on with kindness
Not even the wind blew to remind me of time
Approaches that which they insist on calling happiness
The nightbird says its name

On a tripod made of limbs hoist this vision
At eveningtime when they examine you in love
Glancing back on the road long as sleep
Little girl skipping the owl's hushed way.

THAT STRAIGHTLACED CHRISTIAN
THING BETWEEN HER LEGS

Then I made room
for you in my bed:
my sprig of mint,
my shewolf

—hermit oyster
guarding your precious
garlic-clove,

swarm of black ants,
poultice
against all aches . . .

Always furious
impatient
for the two of us
to get even closer.
My nunnery,
my October.
You are the sugarbowl
the moles keep
at the center
of the earth.

Like a vein of gold
I darted
after you,
sunken,
keen as a claw,

I knew the bees
that make nights
in their hives.

Ink, I went
looking for you
with my quill.
I still need to write my life
in what remains
of this instant.

You were already
a plumtree.
An old woman
kept watch
while the plum
ripened.
I was the woodcutter.
Humming to myself
I honed the ax.
Quickly,
I was the hand
reaching
for a chestnut
in the fire.

Then I was
the seeing-eye dog
leading you
on a leash
of sighs.
But you turned
into a nest,
hushed,
opaque,
all the way out
in the invisible.

55

When you became
a pincushion,
the pins pierced you
sweetly
out of your deep
slumber.
I covered you
with my mouth.
Told you,
little black ember,
skillet
for my heart's
hailstone,
may my touch be
the only dress
you ever wear,

and then again,
in a drone of the one
saying
his bedtime prayer:

woman,
raise your legs high
in the name of
poverty,
and let's make love
slowly
because the bed
creaks.

BREASTS

I love breasts, hard
Full breasts, guarded
By a button.

They come in the night.
The bestiaries of the ancients
Which include the unicorn
Have kept them out.

Pearly, like the east
An hour before sunrise,
Two ovens of the only
Philosopher's stone
Worth bothering about.

They bring on their nipples
Beads of inaudible sighs,
Vowels of delicious clarity
For the little red schoolhouse of our mouths.

Elsewhere, solitude
Makes another gloomy entry
In its ledger, misery
Borrows another cup of rice.

They draw nearer: Animal
Presence. In the barn
The milk shivers in the pail.

I like to come up to them
From underneath, like a kid
Who climbs on a chair
To reach a jar of forbidden jam.

Gently, with my lips,
Loosen the button.
Have them slip into my hands
Like two freshly poured beer-mugs.

I spit on fools who fail to include
Breasts in their metaphysics,
Star-gazers who have not enumerated them
Among the moons of the earth . . .

They give each finger
Its true shape, its joy:
Virgin soap, foam
On which our hands are cleansed.

And how the tongue honors
These two sour buns,
For the tongue is a feather
Dipped in egg-yolk.

I insist that a girl
Stripped to the waist
Is the first and last miracle,

That the old janitor on his deathbed
Who demands to see the breasts of his wife
For one last time
Is the greatest poet who ever lived.

O my sweet, my wistful bagpipes.
Look, everyone is asleep on the earth.

Now, in the absolute immobility
Of time, drawing the waist
Of the one I love to mine,

I will tip each breast
Like a dark heavy grape
Into the hive
Of my drowsy mouth.

THE PLACE

They were talking about the war
The table still uncleared in front of them.
Across the way, the first window
Of the evening was already lit.
He sat, hunched over, quiet,
The old fear coming over him . . .
It grew darker. She got up to take the plate—
Now unpleasantly white—to the kitchen.
Outside in the fields, in the woods
A bird spoke in proverbs,
A Pope went out to meet Attila,
The ditch was ready for its squad.

RETURN TO A PLACE LIT BY
A GLASS OF MILK

Late at night our hands stop working.
They lie open with tracks of animals
Journeying across the fresh snow.
They need no one. Solitude surrounds them.

As they come closer, as they touch,
It is like two small streams
Which upon entering a wide river
Feel the pull of the distant sea.

The sea is a room far back in time
Lit by the headlights of a passing car.
A glass of milk glows on the table.
Only you can reach it for me now.

SOUP

Take a little backache
Melt some snow from the year of your birth
Add the lump in your throat
And the fear of the dark

Instead of oil a pinch of chill
But let it be northern
Instead of parsley
Swear loudly into it

Then stir it with the night
Until its fins and penny-nails
Are blended.

*

On what shall we cook it?

On something like a cough
On the morning star about to fade
On the whisker of a black cat
On an oval locket with a picture of Jesus
On the nipple of a sleeping woman

Let's cook it until we raise
That heavy autumnal cloud
From its bowels
Even if it takes a hundred years.

*

What do you think it will taste like?

Like barbed wire, like burglar's tools
Like a word you'd rather forget
The way the book tastes to the goat
Who is chewing and spitting its pages
Also like the ear of a girl you are about to undress
Also like the rim of a smile

In the twentieth century
We arouse the sun's curiosity
By whistling for the soup
To be served.

*

What in the world shall we eat it with?

With a shoe that left last night
To baptize itself in the rain
With two eyes that quarrel in the same head
With a finger which is the divining-rod
Searching for its clearest streak
With a hat in which the thoughts
Grind each other into black pepper

We'll dive into the soup
With a grain of salt between our teeth
And won't come up
Until we learn its song.

*

And this is what we'll have on the side:

Lust on halfshells with lemon wedges
Mushrooms stuffed with death and almonds
The bread of memory, a black bread
Blood sausages of yes and no

A hiccup in aspic with paprika
Cold wind fried in onions
A roast of darkest thoughts
Young burp with fish ears
Green apples glazed with envy

We'll wash it all down
With the ale brewed from the foam
Gathered at the mouths
Of our old pursuers:
The mad, god-sent, bloodhounds.

V

There's nothing more serious than a joke.

Anonymous

THE CHICKEN WITHOUT A HEAD

for Ron & Lynn Sukenick

When two times two was three,
The chicken without a head was hatched.
When the earth was still flat,
It fell off its edge, daydreaming.
When there were 13 signs in the zodiac,
It found a dead star for its gizzard.
When the first fox was getting married,
It taught itself to fly with one wing.
When all the eggs were still golden,
The clouds in the sky tasted like sweet corn.
When the rain flooded its coop,
Its wishbone was its arc.
Ah, when the chicken used to roast itself,
The lightning was its skewer,
The thunder its baste and salt!

*

The chicken without a head made a sigh,
And then a hailstone out of that sigh,
And a window for the hailstone to strike.
Nine lives it made for itself
And nine coats of solitude to dress them in.
It made its own shadow. No, I'm lying.
It only made a bedbug to bite some holes in the shadow.
Made it all out of nothing. Made a needle
To sew back its broken eggshell.
Made a naked woman—God made the others.
Its father made the knife, but it honed the blade
Until it threw back its image like a funhouse mirror.

Made it all a little at a time.
Who's to say it'd be happier if it didn't?

*

A soldier met the headless chicken
On a lonely street at night
And had his hair turn white.
A preacher met the devil's drumstick
And made the sign of a cross.
A drunk met his guardian angel
And wanted to ride on its back.
A poor widow met her supper
And ran home for a fork and knife.
A birdwatcher met a jailbird
And wrote down the color of its feathers.
A girl met the same trickster
And let it scratch her
Where it didn't itch.
An orphan met the headless one
And hid it under his shirt,
Then in a book,
Then in his pillow.

*

Hear the song of a chicken without a head
As it goes listening to its own droppings:
A song in which two parallel lines
Meet at infinity, in which God
Makes the last of the little apples,
In which the golden fleece is heard growing
On a little girl's pubis. The song
Of swearwords dreaming of a pure mouth.

The song of a doornail raised from the dead.
Equally, the song of joy because accomplices
Have been found, because the egg's safe
In the cuckoo's nest. The only song
You wade into until your hat floats.
A song of contagious laughter.
A lethal song.
That's right, the song of night-vision.

*

Punch my judy and I'll punch yours.
The chicken's in love with the invisible.
Asleep, it writes her love letters.
Sleepless, it sends them tied to a feather.
The earth and the heaven send them back:
No road, no door, no address to the invisible.
    A headless chicken in a headless year
Of a headless week of a headless month,
On a headless evening of a headless day,
Searched for an appropriate engagement ring
Saying over and over and over again:
No finger, no teat, no braid on the invisible . . .
    Randy chicken, the stump of its neck
Like a bloody swollen genital, undressed
Until only its death-rattle was left . . .
The invisible, in the meantime,
Close by, in love with itself.

*

The chicken on fire and the words
Around it like a ring of fabulous beasts.
Each night it threw them a portion of its innards.

The words were hungry. The night, without end.
Whatever our gallows-bird made, the head unmade.
Its long lost, its axed-off head
Yawned in the sky like a winter moon.
Down below the great work went on:
The table that supplies itself with bread,
A saw that cuts a dream in half,
Wings so fast that they won't get wet in heavy rain,
The egg that says to the frying pan:
I swear it by the hair in my yolk,
There's no such thing as a chicken without a head.

*

The chicken without a head ran home to roost.
Alongside a fleeing spark it ran.
Ran over a puddle the color of its blackest feather,
Over one foot in the grave.
Ran under your sister's skirt;
Wildest hope honing the ticks of its heart;
Armies parting to let it pass . . .
Gobbled shudders driven up its spine as it ran.
Deafening silence rose like dust in its wake.
Ran with dropped drawers after a swift word.
Red ink, black ink trickling from its talons.
Ran, leaving its muddy tracks, its crooked scrawl,
Leaving its squinting head far behind.
Time flying elsewhere—ran through a church door,
Through a prison door headless into the thin air.
Ran, and is still running this Good Friday,
Between raindrops, tripping over its puns,
Hellfoxes on its trail.